Anonymous

Lowell's tribute to her returned soldiers of the Spanish-American war

1898

Anonymous

Lowell's tribute to her returned soldiers of the Spanish-American war
1898

ISBN/EAN: 9783337133962

Printed in Europe, USA, Canada, Australia, Japan

Cover: Foto ©ninafisch / pixelio.de

More available books at **www.hansebooks.com**

Flag of the brave!
Thy stars have seen
As noble deeds as e'er hath been.
Thy blue, to every sky unrolled,
No tale of shame
Hath ever told.
May thy bold stripes forever be
Restraining bars to Tyranny.
      F. G. Rose.

Lowell's Tribute

to her returned Soldiers
of the Spanish-American
War, 1898
Co. M, 9th Regiment
Co.'s C and G, 6th Regiment
M. V. M.
at the Armory
November 30, 1898

"Each of the heroes around us has
    fought for his land and line,
But thou hast fought for a stranger in
    hate of a wrong not thine.
Happy are all free people, too strong to
    be dispossessed,
But blest are those among nations who
    dare to be strong for the rest."

Breathes there a man with soul so dead,
Who never to himself hath said,
   This is my own, my native land!
Whose heart hath ne'er within him burned,
As home his footsteps he hath turned,
   From wandering on a foreign strand!

A Prayer.

And in thy majesty ride prosperously, because of truth and meekness and righteousness; and thy right hand shall teach thee terrible things. — Psalm xlv : 4.

Almighty God! eternal source
   Of every arm we dare to wield,
Be Thine the thanks, as Thine the force,
   On reeling deck or stricken field;
The thunder of the battle hour
Is but the whisper of Thy power.

By Thee was given the thought that bowed
   All hearts upon the victor deck,
When high above the battle's shroud
   The white flag fluttered o'er the wreck,
And Thine the hand that checked the cheer
In that wild hour of death and fear.

O Lord of Love! be Thine the grace
   To teach, amid the wrath of war,
Sweet pity for a humbled race,
   Some thought of those in lands afar,
Where sad-eyed women vainly yearn
For those who never shall return.

Great Master of earth's mighty school
   Whose children are of every land!
Inform with love our alien rule,
   And stay us with Thy warning hand,
If, tempted by imperial greed,
We in Thy watchful eyes exceed —

That in the days to come, O Lord!
   When we ourselves have passed away,
And all are gone who drew the sword,
   The children of our breed may say,
These were our sires who, doubly great,
Could strike yet spare the fallen state.

— S. Weir Mitchell.

MEN WHO MADE HISTORY.

EXECUTIVE MANSION
WASHINGTON
November 19, 1898.

Mr. Alfred E. Rose,
  Chairman Banquet Committee,
  Lowell, Mass.

Dear Sir:

I have learned with pleasure of the celebration to be held on the 30th instant by the citizens of Lowell in honor of the Sixth and Ninth Regiments, Massachusetts Volunteer Infantry, who have recently returned from the victorious campaigns in Cuba and Porto Rico.

Please convey to those present on this patriotic occasion, and especially to the soldiers themselves, my hearty appreciation of the gallant and faithful services which they rendered to their country.

Very truly yours,

LEADING GENERALS OF THE WAR.

The Causes Which Led up to the War.

"REMEMBER THE MAINE."

*I*T may be of interest to review the various courses of action on the part of our Government proposed and discussed during the last three years,—recognition of Cuban belligerency, recognition of Cuban independence, intervention.

When, in the first quarter of this century, Mexico and Central America, Venezuela, New Granada (United States of Columbia), Ecuador, Peru, Chili, and the other Spanish possessions in South America threw off the Spanish yoke, Cuba remained loyal, and gained for herself the title of "The Ever-faithful Isle." One would naturally suppose that Spain would have rewarded her for her fidelity, instead of curtailing whatever privileges she had before enjoyed. The latter course was taken, however, and the loyalty of Cuba gradually became a thing of the past. Before the present one there have been four insurrections in the last seventy years,—1829, 1848-51, 1855, and the bitter ten years' war, 1868-78. The last was ended with a compromise and the promise of reforms which were never carried into substantial effect, and the Cubans began their present revolt in February, 1895, somewhat less than four years ago. During this time, as well as during the 1868-78 war, the United States Government has faithfully observed its obligations as a friendly nation, and, except for the moral pressure that has been brought to bear and official declarations that a time might come when the interests of humanity would force us to interfere, Spain has been permitted, so far as our Government has been concerned, to take absolutely her own course in Cuba.

Our country deserves neither praise nor blame for this; she has simply been doing her duty as one of the family of nations. Many sympathizers with Cuba have been disposed to scoff at international law, but they forget that its principles have been established as the result of the combined experience of the great civilized nations of the world. To observe them is incumbent upon all governments alike, and in the end, however hard it may be in any special case, to observe them strictly is in the highest interest of all alike.

Recognition of Cuban belligerency was early urged upon our Government. To grant it would have required the further declaration that the Government of the United States would "maintain a strict neutrality between the contending powers," thus putting the insurgents in their relation to our Government upon a par with Spain. Before such action can be taken without violation of the principles of international law, what is called "public war" must exist. Nobody questions that a war has been going on in Cuba for the last three years, but it has been of the nature of guerrilla warfare. For civil war to become public war, "the insurgents must present the aspect of a political community or 'de facto' power, having a certain coherence and a certain independence of position, in respect of territorial limits, of population, of interests, and of destiny." It has not been proved that the Cuban insurgents have at any time presented this aspect, and both President Grant in the ten years' war and President McKinley now have deemed recognition of their belligerency inadmissible. As a matter of fact, recognition, by and of itself, could have done the insurgents no practical good. It would have conferred upon both "powers" certain rights of "visit and search on the seas and seizure of vessels and cargoes and contraband of war," etc., but, since the insurgents had no navy, to confer them could benefit only Spain. Profit to the insurgents could be derived only from the war with the United States almost sure to come, sooner or later, from the inevitable friction between the two governments arising from the exercise of these rights by Spain.

Recognition of the independence of a new government is recognition of a fact, not an expression of sympathy. It is so generally understood that the essentials of an independent state are lacking in this case that recognition of the independence of Cuba has found comparatively few supporters. President Grant in the ten years' war pronounced it, in his opinion, "impracticable and indefensible," and President McKinley in his last annual message declared that, in his judgment, that opinion is equally applicable to the situation today.

Intervention to end the war remains to be considered. A universally recognized principle of international law, based, we must remember, upon what has been proved to be necessary for self-protection and the maintenance of the peace of the world, rigidly limits the right of military intervention by one nation in the internal affairs of another. With a single exception, such interference is justified only by "the necessary self-defense of a nation's material interests or of the national honor, which is its highest interest. . . . It is too well settled to admit of dispute that the inconvenience and loss suffered by the commerce of neutral states when war exists, though often considerable, constitute no ground for intervention, but must be borne." The high authority whom we have just been quoting says that the sole exception to the principle stated above is "where to prevent unjustifiable slaughter and outrage in another country, it [intervention] becomes absolutely necessary." Here, then, if anywhere, we must find justification for forcible interference. What are the facts?

Reports from both sides were exaggerated and false, and it was very hard to learn the truth. But we know that there is no such thing as merciful war. War is necessarily brutal; it implies killing and maiming and laying waste. All these things, and more, are permitted by the rules of civilized warfare, and so long as non-combatants were not interfered with there was little to choose between the Spaniards and the insurgents. Both sides were guilty of atrocities, but neither to such an extent as to justify outside interference. A change came with the issuance of General Weyler's concentration order towards the end of 1896. This was directed against non-combatants, chiefly old men, women, and children. The country regions of the island had been ravaged by both sides alike; industries of every kind, agricultural and other, had been stopped, and the forces of the insurgents had been greatly increased by the consequent lack of employment. Nearly all able-bodied young men had gone to join them, leaving behind chiefly their aged fathers and mothers, helpless wives and sisters and little children. It was against these that General Weyler issued his infamous order: "That all the inhabitants of the country districts, or those who reside outside the lines of fortifications of the towns, shall, within the period of eight days, concentrate themselves in the towns which are occupied by the troops. Any individual found outside in the country at the expiration of this period shall be considered a rebel, and shall be dealt with as such." These, then, are the "reconcentrados," whose condition, as he personally saw it in his recent visit to Cuba, we will let United States Senator Proctor describe. He tells us that outside of Havana, where everything seems to go on much as usual, what one sees "is not peace, nor is it war. It is desolation and distress, misery and starvation. Every town and village is surrounded by a trocha (trench), . . . the dirt being thrown up in the inside and a barbed wire fence on the outer side of the trench. These trochas have, at every corner and at frequent intervals along the sides, what are called forts, but which are really small blockhouses, many of them more like a large sentry-box, loopholed for musketry and with a guard of from two to ten soldiers in each.

"The purpose of these trochas is to keep the reconcentrados in, as well as to keep the insurgents out. From all the surrounding country the people have been driven into these fortified towns, and held there to subsist as they can. They are virtually prison-yards and not unlike one in general appearance, except that the walls are not so high and strong; but they suffice, where every point is in range of a soldier's rifle, to keep in the poor reconcentrado women and children." When the order was issued many doubtless did not learn of it within the eight days allowed them. "Others failed to grasp its terrible meaning. Its execution was left to the guerrillas to drive in all that had not obeyed, and I was informed that in many cases a torch was applied to their homes, with no notice, and the inmates fled with such clothing as they might have on, their stock and other belongings being appropriated by the guerrillas. When they reached the town they were allowed to build huts of palm leaves in the suburbs and vacant places within the trochas, and left to live if they could. Their huts are about ten by fifteen feet in size, and for want of space are usually crowded together very closely. They have no floor but the ground, and no furniture, and after a year's wear but little clothing, except such stray substitutes as they can extemporize. With large families, or with more than one in this little space, the commonest sanitary provisions are impossible. Conditions are unmentionable in this respect. Torn from their homes, with foul earth, foul air, foul water, and foul food or none, what wonder that one-half have died and that one-quarter of the living are so diseased that they cannot be saved? A form of dropsy is a common disorder resulting from these conditions. Little children are still walking about with arms and chest terribly emaciated, eyes swollen, and abdomen bloated to three times its natural size. The physicians say these cases are hopeless.

"Deaths in the streets have not been uncommon. I was told by one of our consuls that people had been found dead about the markets in the morning, where they had crawled, hoping to get some stray bits of food from the early hucksters, and that there had been cases where they had dropped dead inside the market, surrounded by food. These people were independent and self-supporting before Weyler's order."

The character of Senator Proctor is such as to guarantee the truth of his statement of what he saw and heard. Should not the death by starvation of two hundred thousand non-combatants and the reduction to their present condition of as many more, through the execution of the Spanish general's order, be considered the "unjustifiable slaughter and outrage" which, by international law, makes intervention necessary? And the colonial policy of Spain being what it is and always has been, and her faithlessness to promises made to end the war of 1868-78 being borne in mind, can it be believed that any intervention would have been effective which did not result in the complete withdrawal of Spain from the island?

President McKinley had the feeling of a majority of the people of the United States with him when he concluded his reply to the address of the foreign ambassadors in Washington on April 7 by a declaration of the determination of our Government "to fulfil a duty to humanity by ending a situation the indefinite prolongation of which has become insufferable."

According to their deeds, accordingly he will repay, fury to his adversaries, recompense to his enemies; to the islands he will repay recompense. —Isaiah lix: 18.

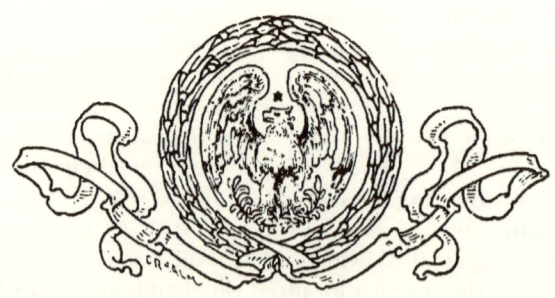

Cuba.

What sounds arouse me from my slumbers light?
  "Land ho! all hands, ahoy!" — I'm on the deck:
'Tis early dawn; the day-star yet is bright,
  A few white vapory bars the zenith fleck,
And, lo! along the horizon, bold and high,
  The purple hills of Cuba! Hail! all hail!
Isle of undying verdure, with thy sky
  Of purest azure! Welcome, odorous gale!
O scene of life and joy! thou art arrayed
  In hues of unimagined loveliness.
Sing louder, brave old mariner! and aid
  My swelling heart its rapture to express;
For from enchanted memory never more
Shall fade this dawn sublime, this fair, resplendent shore.
                            — *Epes Sargent.*

GENERAL NELSON A. MILES,
Commanding General of the Armies of the United States.

HEADQUARTERS OF THE ARMY,
WASHINGTON, D.C.

Nov. 21, 1898.

Alfred E. Rose, Esq.,
　　Lowell, Mass.

Dear Sir:

　　I am in receipt of yours of the 17th informing me of the proposed banquet to be tendered to the members of the 6th and 9th regiments of Massachusetts Volunteers, and I trust that the function will prove a success in every way *such as* will be gratifying to all concerned.

　　　　　Very truly yours,

　　　　　　Nelson A. Miles
　　　　　　　Major General
　　　　　　　　Commanding

GENERAL WILLIAM R. SHAFTER,
who commanded the Santiago campaign.

The Siege and Capture of Santiago.

*T*HE first campaign of the army in Cuba lasted a month, and was in every respect as brilliant and, except in the severe losses we have experienced, as fortunate as the remarkable successes of the navy. We won a decided victory and obtained the surrender of one-tenth of the soil of Cuba, with two fine harbors and twenty thousand or twenty-five thousand of the Spanish troops. Strange as it may seem, this was the first campaign ever fought by the regular army of the United States with volunteers assisting. In all our other wars the volunteers have formed the principal strength of the army, in which the regulars played a subordinate part numerically, however distinguished in conduct.

The month of June was notable for the first landing of troops in Cuba and the first land battles of the war. On the tenth of that month a body of marines, about six hundred strong, under command of Lieutenant-Colonel Huntington, landed without opposition at Guantanamo, a fine port about fifty miles east of Santiago Bay. It is the most easterly of the good harbors on the south coast of Cuba. Camp was established on a hill overlooking the bay, and there the marines were attacked on the eleventh by a force of Spaniards said to number more than fifteen hundred men, who were driven off after a sharp fight. At first there were stories of carelessness in picketing the camp, but our subsequent experience at Santiago has shown that the thick and thorny underbrush of the Cuban soil gives remarkable advantages to a wily and creeping foe. It presents conditions of scout and picket duty that seem to be somewhat novel; for even our regulars, many of whom have fought the Indians, had to learn its peculiarities by experience and at some loss. Fighting was more or less constant until the fourteenth, when we made our counter attack and drove off the enemy once for all time. Our losses were six killed and ten wounded. The Spaniards seem to have lost one hundred or more.

This was our first experience of wounds made with the small-caliber, swift-moving, long-range bullets, and their shattering effects gave rise to stories that the enemy was using explosives; but wounded Spaniards show that our own Krag-Joergensen rifle produces the same effects.

The Cubans gave us effective aid in these fights, and lost heavily. Thirty of their wounded were cared for on our hospital ship, the "Solace." They were about one thousand strong at Guantanamo.

General Shafter, after many trying delays, left Tampa, Fla., on June 14, with a fleet of thirty-five transports, carrying sixteen

REAL ARMY LIFE.

thousand men, and convoyed by fourteen warships. It was the largest expedition in our history, and the largest anywhere since the Crimean War, forty-four years ago. The voyage was made slowly to allow all the transports to keep with the fleet, which did not arrive off Santiago until June 20. The use of steam exclusively permitted the fleet to move with a uniformity of alignment that probably has not been seen since the old days of galleys. The transports moved in three lines, one thousand feet apart, and with an interval of six hundred feet between the ships of each line. War vessels were stationed on each flank of the transports, and the whole fleet covered the sea for eight miles in length and one in breadth. Sailing along the north coast of Cuba, it rounded Cape Maysi, the eastern extremity of the island, and turned westward along the south coast to the vicinity of Santiago de Cuba, which it reached at noon on June 20. The weather was excellent throughout the voyage.

On the twenty-second the landing was made, and Admiral Sampson's order, issued the day before, disclosed the following plan of operations: A strong feint of landing was made at Cabanas, two and one-half miles west of Santiago Bay, where the Spaniards had one of their most effective batteries. The "Texas," "Scorpion," and "Vixen" ran in and engaged this battery, while ten of the transports, ranged two miles from the shore, occupied themselves busily in lowering boats and hoisting them on board again. At the same time a body of five hundred Cubans made a demonstration west of the place. All this was done to draw the attention of the Spaniards away from the coast east of Santiago Bay, where, at Baiquiri, Altares, and Aguadores, other ships of the fleet were engaged in shelling the shore. The actual landing took place at Baiquiri, twelve miles east of the bay. At that point there is a well-built iron pier five hundred feet long, the property of an American mining company, and also a wooden dock. The dock was an invaluable aid in landing, and the iron pier afterwards served an equally useful purpose in landing the artillery and stores.

Three small steamers were ordered to prepare for towing boats. Each had two tow-lines, one on each side, long enough for a dozen or more boats, and the latter were drawn both from the transports and from seven of the largest vessels in the fleet. Also all the steam cutters and launches from the latter vessels were sent to assist. These arrangements were so well planned and carried out that six thousand men and considerable necessary stores were landed the first day without accident, forming a scene that is described as most enlivening. The Spaniards did not oppose the landing seriously, and the only losses suffered on our side were one Cuban and one man on the "Texas" killed, and eight wounded. All of the American losses were caused by one shell fired from the Socapa battery, on the west side of Santiago Bay, which was engaged by the "Texas."

Our Cuban allies aided the operations materially. They had been supplied with arms and ammunition, and, besides the demonstration at the west flank of our operations, they held the country on the east, between Santiago and Guantanamo. They numbered in all about five thousand seven hundred men. During the next two days the remainder of the force was landed, with artillery and a large quantity of ammunition and stores, but two men were crushed by boats and killed.

BURNING SIBONEY.

The steadiness and freedom from loss with which this embarkation of an army proceeded should not blind us to the fact that it was a hazardous operation carried out upon a coast well guarded by fortifications and in the face of an enemy who has shown himself to be possessed of fighting qualities of a very high order. In preparing to resist insurgent attacks the Spaniards have built innumerable blockhouses along the coast, and the presence of our fleet in this neighborhood for a month or more had led them to increase these means of defense by batteries and trenches. It was known that in this part of Cuba there were from fifteen thousand to thirty thousand Spanish troops besides the men of Admiral Cervera's squadron, and there was every reason to believe that our landing would be resisted hotly. We found that every road to Santiago had been entrenched, and it is probable that the Spaniards expected to oppose us at the seashore; but we exhibited a strength that it was hopeless to combat. The most powerful fleet the world has ever seen in fighting trim was gathered on the coast of Cuba and covered it for twenty miles with a steady fire, which could have risen to destructive proportions at any point where it was needed.

Much confusion in the early accounts of the operations was caused by the fact that one name is often used on the Cuban coast for two distinct places: first, for a town which may be from one to three miles inland, and, second, for a point on the coast where the landing-place for that town is established. Thus Demajayabo, the inland town, and Ensenada Demajayabo, the bay which forms the landing nearest to the town. Baiquiri, Juragua, and Aguadores all have the same double significance. Baiquiri is a village about one and one-half miles from the landing-place of the same name and seventeen miles from Santiago. Back of it is a high plateau, and beyond that a road which we expected to find practicable for artillery, but which proved to be in bad condition. Our troops moved up from the landing to Baiquiri village, and, in fact, to Demajayabo, two miles northwest of that place, the day they landed; and some of them were able to sleep under roof the first night, as the enemy had evacuated these places too hastily to destroy them entirely. From Demajayabo the road runs through Altares, Juraguasito, and Sevilla to Santiago.

Besides the main landing at Baiquiri, two other landing-places on the coast between Santiago Bay and Baiquiri were occupied. These are Siboney, where the iron company's railroad reaches the sea, and Aguadores, within two or three miles of Morro Castle, where the railroad leaves the coast and turns in toward Santiago. Here it crosses a high iron trestle and bridge, which was blown up by the Spaniards, and which is also covered by some of the best-manned batteries of the enemy. Under these conditions no serious attempt was made to follow up the line of the railroad.

The day after landing the troops moved forward from Demajayabo to Juragua, on the railroad, and a little beyond this place the Spaniards suddenly appeared in some force, but were driven back by our advance force of Americans and Cubans.

From Juragua the column advanced toward Sevilla, and one and one-half miles east of this town, at La Guasima, our troops felt the first serious resistance of the Spaniards and suffered their first loss. Our force, nine hundred and twenty-four strong, was com-

A SOLDIER'S SHELTER.

manded by Colonel Young, and consisted of parts of the Twenty-third United States Infantry, First and Tenth United States Cavalry, and First Volunteer Cavalry, the latter being commonly known as "Roosevelt's Rough Riders." The latter formed the left of the line, the regulars being on the right. The attack was made by our men at daylight, and after an hour's sharp fighting the enemy gave way. In this action the troops were obliged to charge a superior and well-posted force supplied with two machine guns, supposed to have been obtained from Admiral Cervera's fleet. The strength of the Spaniards is not known accurately, but is thought to have been more than fifteen hundred men. Our loss, as given officially by General Wheeler, was sixteen killed and fifty-two wounded. Forty-two of the casualties were in the Rough Riders and twenty-six in the regular cavalry. This engagement attracted great attention, being the first in which the army was engaged. It is known as the battle of Siboney, La Quasina (or La Guasima).

The plan of advance from the seacoast was to send forward Cubans as scouts, with small detachments of our own men in close touch with them, while the main body followed. The enemy fell back at all points until the right of our line was within about three miles of Santiago, and by the end of June the two armies had defined their positions. At Aguadores—not the landing-place, but the town, two and one-half miles inland—was the right of the Spanish position, behind which, and two or three miles to the rear, was Morro Castle and its strong outworks. North of this place they had entrenchments across the railroad, and from that point east and northward around the city, at a distance of three or four miles from it. Some of the principal points were well fortified. Our line was at first about five miles long, but it was lengthened continually to the right for the purpose of enclosing the city completely and cutting off all retreat. Of the sixteen thousand men in our army, probably three-fourths were on the battle line, which became very thin in places as the advance toward the north was made. The country around Santiago is very broken, offering decided advantages to a defender and preventing cooperative tactics on the part of our divisions. Each force went for the enemy in its front and could expect little help from its neighbors.

A week was consumed in these operations and in landing and sending forward the artillery. The engineers worked hard to transform the foot-path to a wagon road, throw bridges over streams and ravines, and open roads through the jungle for the artillery. The ships of Admiral Sampson's fleet made repeated attempts to find and cut the telegraph cable, which was so sunk in the ocean ooze as to make the task very difficult. At length the French cable was picked up, telegraph and telephone lines run out to the front and connected with Playa del Este, a place east of Baiquiri, and with Guantanamo by the shore cable, until at length our front was in full telephonic connection with headquarters and these by direct cable with Washington. The engineers also cut the pipe line that conveyed water to Santiago and turned it to the supply of our own men. This did not deprive the city absolutely of water, which would be impossible in this rainy season.

The disposition of our troops was as follows: The army of invasion comprised the Fifth Army Corps under Major-General W. R. Shafter and was composed of two divisions of infantry, two brigades of cavalry, and two brigades of light and four batteries of heavy artillery. General Lawton commanded the Sec-

THE WATER SUPPLY, CUBA.

ond Division, operating on the right, where the capture of El Caney was his principal task, and had the brigades of General Chaffee, the Seventh, Twelfth, and Seventeenth Infantry; General Ludlow, Eighth and Twenty-second Infantry and Second Massachusetts Volunteers; and Colonel Miles, First, Fourth, and Twenty-fifth Infantry. In the center General Kent commanded the First Division, consisting of General Hawkins' brigade, the

Sixth and Sixteenth Infantry and Seventy-first New York Volunteers; Colonel Pearson's brigade, the Second, Tenth, and Twenty-first Infantry; and Colonel Wikoff's brigade, the Ninth, Thirteenth, and Twenty-fourth Infantry. General Wheeler's cavalry division contained two brigades, Colonel Sumner's, the Third, Sixth, and Ninth Cavalry, and Colonel Young's, the First and Tenth Cavalry and First Volunteer Cavalry. The cavalry operated at both the two principal points of attack, but fought dismounted, no horses having been shipped. At the end of the first day's fighting General Kent was reenforced by General Bates with the Third and Twentieth Infantry, coming up from the coast. On the left General Duffield engaged Aguadores with the Twenty-third and part of the Thirty-fourth Michigan, and a force of about two thousand Cubans. Grimes' and Best's batteries of artillery were with the center and Capron's and Parkhouse's were with General Lawton on the right. General Shafter, General Joseph Wheeler, our old antagonist in the Civil War, and General Young were all too ill to be in the field, though General Wheeler did go out in an ambulance. Headquarters were at Sevilla.

The declared purpose of General Shafter was to attack as soon as possible, for the risks of the Cuban climate to Northern men, exposed to a furious sun through the days and compelled to sleep through the chill nights with poor shelter, were at least as great as anything that could be expected from the Spanish fire.

The attack began on July 1, and involved the whole line, but the principal battle took place at the hill town of San Juan, opposite our center, and at El Caney, a little place on the right of our line. El Caney was taken by General Lawton's men after a sharp contest and severe loss on both sides. Here as everywhere there were blockhouses and trenches to be carried in the face of a hot fire from Mauser rifles, and the rifles were well served. The jungle must disturb the aim seriously, for our men did not suffer severely while under its cover, but in crossing clearings the rapid fire of the repeating rifles told with deadly effect. The object of the attack on El Caney was to crush the Spanish lines at a point near the city and allow us to gain a high hill from which the place could be bombarded if necessary. In all of this we were entirely successful. The engagement began at 6.40 A. M., and by four o'clock the Spaniards were forced to abandon the place and retreat toward their lines nearer the city. The fight was opened by Capron's battery, at a range of twenty-four hundred yards, and the troops engaged were Chaffee's brigade, the Seventh, Twelfth, and Seventeenth Infantry, who moved on Caney from the east;

Colonel Miles' brigade of the First, Fourth, and Twenty-fifth Infantry, operating from the south; while Ludlow's brigade, containing the Eighth and Twenty-second Infantry and Second Massachusetts, made a detour to attack from the southwest.

The operations of our center were calculated to cut the communications of Santiago with El Morro and permit our forces to advance to the bay, and the principal effort of General Linares, the Spanish commander in the field, seems to have been to defeat this movement. He had fortified San Juan strongly, throwing up on it entrenchments that in the hands of a more determined force would have been impregnable.

The battle at San Juan was opened by Grimes' battery, to which the enemy replied with shrapnel. The cavalry, dismounted, supported by Hawkins' brigade, advanced up the valley from the hill of El Pozo, forded several streams, where they lost heavily, and deployed at the foot of the series of hills known as San Juan under a sharp fire from all sides, which was exceedingly annoying because the enemy could not be discerned, owing to the long range and smokeless powder. They were under fire for two hours before the charge could be made and a position reached under the brow of the hill. It was not until nearly four o'clock that the neighboring hills were occupied by our troops and the final successful effort to crown the ridge could be made. The obstacles interposed by the Spaniards made these charges anything but the "rushes" which war histories mention so often. They were slow and painful advances through difficult obstacles and withering fire. The last "charge" lasted an hour, but at 4.45 the fire ceased, with San Juan in our possession.

The Spaniards made liberal use of barbed-wire fencing, which proved to be so effective as a stop to our advance that it is likely to take its place among approved defensive materials in future wars. It was used in two ways: wires were stretched near the ground to trip up our men when on the run. Beyond them were fences in parallel lines, some being too high to be vaulted over. The wires were laid so close together that they had to be separated before an ordinary wire-cutter could be forced between them. These defenses were laid in cultivated valleys and other open spaces which lay under the fire of the entrenchments, and the tree-tops around the clearings were alive with the enemy. Every fence compelled a momentary halt on the part of our men, and during those moments they were exposed to a pitiless fire from all sides. It is not only the strength of the wire and the sharp barbs that make this material so effective for entanglements and obstacles, but the fact that it offers no impediment to the flight of bullets. Short as the halt may be, the assaulting party is fully exposed to a rain of shot from quick-firing rifles at ranges that are known to the defenders.

The object of our attack was a blockhouse on the top of the hill of San Juan, guarded by trenches and the defenses spoken of, one and one-half miles long. Our troops advanced steadily against a hot fire maintained by the enemy, who used their rifles with accuracy, but did not cling to their works stubbornly when we reached them. San Juan was carried in the afternoon. The attack on Aguadores was also successful, though it was not intended to be more than a feint to draw off men who might otherwise have increased our difficulties at San Juan. By nightfall General Shafter was able to telegraph that he had carried all the outworks and was within three-quarters of a mile of the city.

Though the enemy's lines were broken in the principal places, they yielded no more than was forced from them, and the battle was resumed on the 2d. The last day saw our left flank resting on the bay and our lines drawn around the city within easy gun-fire. Fears were entertained that the enemy would evacuate the place, and the right flank was pushed around to the north and eventually to the northwest of the city.

These operations extended the lines so much that the need of more troops to hold them was felt immediately, and General Shafter telegraphed for reenforcements, which were hurried forward, six thousand men reaching him within eight days after the battle. With these the lines were extended still further around the city, which was completely invested from Caimes on the northwest to the bay south of Santiago. Siege-guns were brought up and placed in position, reenforcements of field artillery arrived, entrenchments were thrown up, and every preparation made for a quick reduction of the place by bombardment.

On Sunday, July 3, Admiral Cervera tried to run past the American fleet, but lost all his vessels and was taken prisoner, with seventeen hundred men. His vessels had taken an active part in the battles of the previous two days, shelling our positions with effect.

On July 3, also, General Shafter demanded the surrender of Santiago on pain of bombardment. The demand was refused by General Jose Toral, commanding in the city, and in the interests of humanity General Shafter informed him that the bombardment would be postponed from ten o'clock on the morning of the 4th until noon of the 5th. Several thousand refugees left the city and

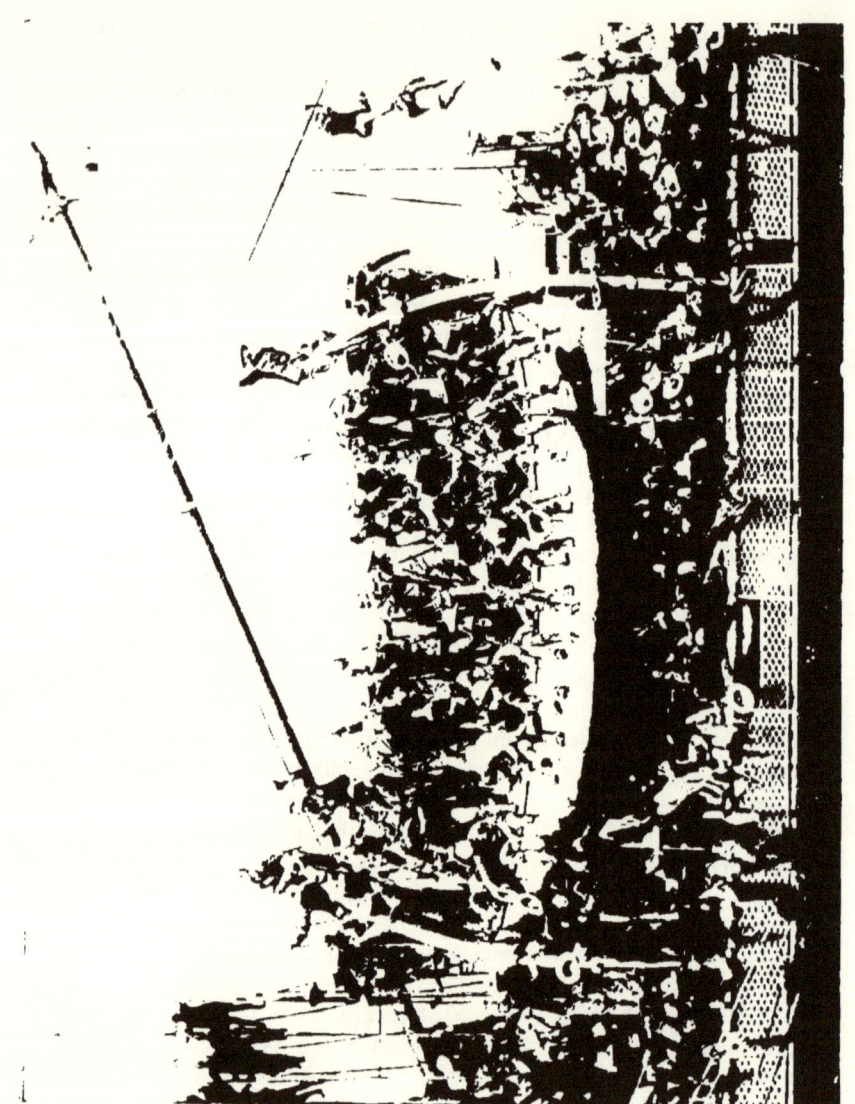

TRANSPORT WITH NINTH MASSACHUSETTS ABOARD.

came into our lines. Others were taken out by various foreign warships which entered the harbor for that purpose. At General Toral's request the cable operators were sent back to enable him to refer the demand for surrender to the authorities at Madrid. General Toral offered to evacuate the city, provided he were permitted to do so with men and arms. This was refused by General Shafter. These negotiations lasted until July 11, when a bombardment of the town was begun by the fleet at a range of four and one half-miles, which lasted two days. The city was not visible from the vessels, which had to stand off shore far enough to enable them to fire over a range of hills intervening. One shell struck a church used as a magazine, which blew up. Otherwise the operation is not thought to have been very effective. The land batteries did not attempt serious bombardment, but shelled the trenches in front of the city.

General Miles arrived on the first day of bombardment, having left Tampa on the 8th. Renewed demands for surrender were made, and after several days' negotiations General Shafter telegraphed on the 14th that General Toral would surrender not only Santiago, "but all of eastern Cuba from Acerraderos on the south to Sagua la Tamana on the north, via Palma, with practically the Fourth Army Corps." This despatch seems to have been premature, for the commissioners who met to draw up the stipulations could not agree, and it was not until the 16th that the following terms were reached: (1) Twenty thousand refugees to go back to Santiago; (2) an American infantry patrol on roads surrounding the city; (3) our hospital corps to give attention to sick and wounded Spanish soldiers; (4) all Spanish troops in the province of Santiago except the ten thousand at Holguin under command of General Luque to come to the city to surrender; (5) the guns and defenses of Santiago to be turned over to the Americans in good condition; (6) the Americans to have full use of the Juragua Railroad; (7) Spanish troops to surrender their arms; (8) all Spaniards to be conveyed to Spain and to take portable church property; (9) Spaniards to cooperate with Americans in destroying harbor mines.

This surrender covered the same territory that was described in the first despatch, which General Toral surrendered as commander-in-chief of the Fourth Army Corps, to which the defense of all eastern Cuba was confided. It contains about four thousand square miles, or one-tenth of the island of Cuba, and probably twenty thousand to twenty-five thousand Spanish troops. It gave us control of the eastern end of Cuba, the fine harbors of Santiago and Guantanamo, and one of the most healthful and, in peace, prosperous districts in Cuba.

On July 17 General Shafter sent the following despatch announcing the formal surrender of Santiago. It is the first despatch of the kind received at Washington from a foreign country in more than fifty years:

"I have the honor to announce that the American flag has been this instant, 12 noon, hoisted over the house of the civil government in the city of Santiago. An immense concourse of people was present, a squadron of cavalry and a regiment of infantry presenting arms, and a band playing national airs. A light battery fired a salute of twenty-one guns.

"Perfect order is being maintained by the municipal government. The distress is very great, but there is little sickness in town and scarcely any yellow fever.

"A small gunboat and about two hundred seamen left by Cervera have surrendered to me. Obstructions are being removed from the mouth of the harbor.

"Upon coming into the city I discovered a perfect entanglement of defenses. Fighting as the Spaniards did the first day, it would have cost five thousand lives to have taken it.

"Battalions of Spanish troops have been depositing arms since daylight in the armory, over which I have a guard. General Toral formally surrendered the plaza and all stores at 9 A. M."

About seven thousand rifles, six hundred thousand cartridges, and many fine modern guns were given up.

This important victory, with its substantial fruits of conquest, was won by a loss of 1593 men, killed, wounded, and missing. Lawton, who had the severe fighting around El Caney, lost 410 men. Kent lost 859 men in the still more severe assault on San Juan and the other conflicts of the center. The cavalry lost 285 men, many of whom fell at El Caney, and the feint at Aguadores cost thirty-seven men. One man of the Signal Corps was killed, and one wounded. Trying as it is to bear the casualties of the first fight, there can be no doubt that in a military sense our success was not dearly won.

Great interest in the work of our troops has been aroused by the fact that in our army there are regiments armed with the newest high-power, smokeless-powder rifles fighting side by side with others who fire the old Springfield rifle, shooting black powder. The results are said to be altogether in favor of the former. The Spaniards use smokeless powder only, but would have no advantage of our men were it not for the black-powder smoke from the volunteers that reveals the position of the troops. It is significant that General Kent, who lost 859 men, had three regiments of volunteers, while General Lawton, who lost 410 men, had only one. Of course the fighting did not present the same difficulty in both cases, but probably the folly of arming a part of the troops with the old Springfield is chargeable with much of our loss. It is reported that the regulars dread to see the volunteers near them, knowing that the smoke from the latter's guns will cost them both dear.

Thus closes the first campaign ever fought by the regular army of the United States. There were twenty-three regiments from the army and five from the volunteers engaged in this battle. Never before has the United States fought with an army principally composed of trained soldiers, and there can be no doubt that we owe our success to their discipline as much as to their valor. The volunteers are reported to have exhibited equal courage and surprising adaptability to the novel conditions of warfare. They fall short of the regulars only in those particulars that are not gained except by long-continued instruction.

—*John A. Church.*

The Story of Company M.

WHEN the details of the story of Company M, Ninth Massachusetts Volunteers, are forgotten, these facts will still be remembered to the honor of the men concerned: Not a single member of the company was missing when, by forced marches, the regiment reached the firing line before Santiago, and not a man faltered on the night following when, aroused from a needed sleep, the regiment was ordered forward to repulse the Spanish charge.

Also to their credit, if there be merit in doing a plain, hungry, sweaty duty, it can be said that the Lowell men of the Ninth went to war in their shirt-sleeves, and nearly all returned in ambulances.

Company M left Lowell on the fourth of May, 1898, and joined the Ninth Regiment in Boston. The commissioned officers of the company were Captain Anthony D. Mitten, First Lieutenant Joseph Gillow, and Second Lieutenant Philip McNulty. The regiment was mustered into the United States service at Camp Dewey, South Framingham, and on May 31 it left the State for Camp Alger, Virginia. There had been the enthusiasm of the hour as the troops were hurried South, but there was a suggestion of active service in the five-mile march that preceded the arrival of the regiment in its new camp. The weather was very hot, but not a Lowell man was lost on the way.

The camp was a pleasant one, and the health of the men was good. On June 13 Lieutenant Gillow took the company to Fairfax Court House and back, a march of thirteen miles, and on the eighteenth the regiment made a march of twenty miles. It had then been demonstrated that the men from Lowell could walk.

The Ninth was attached to General Duffield's brigade, and on June 24 was ordered to proceed to Newport News. A day later the regiment had arrived there and was embarking on the transport "Harvard," which sailed for Cuba on the twenty-sixth. There was no sickness on board, but a healthy interest in the coming campaign.

Sampson's fleet was sighted on the thirtieth, and a few hours later the regiment was landing in small boats off Siboney, Cuba. That night the Ninth made a forced march to the front. The night was very dark, and the way was new. The road led over the hills, through brush and across rivers. There were rumors of a serious fight the night before, and after the first few miles of the march limping evidences of it were met, as the wounded passed slowly to the rear.

Then there came a place where Company M saw the first dead of the war. There were bodies lying beside the road. There was light enough to see them, and men in the ranks of the Lowell

COLONEL BOGAN.

company faltered as if they would go over to look at the men who had been under fire and were now silent where they fought. "You can't do the dead any good," said the captain of the company, and the men fell into step again. Their faces were white, and a few of them drawn, but they never showed signs of leaving the column again.

Daybreak came. There was a hissing in the air and the roar of a battery a mile away; and, throwing away their rolls, their two days' rations, and their heavy blue coats, the Lowell men went

OFFICERS OF NINTH MASSACHUSETTS.
Colonel Bogan, Lieutenant-Colonel Logan, Major Grady, Adjutant Kelly, Surgeon Devine, and Quartermaster Fennessy.

orderly hurried by with the news that the Spanish were attacking. The captain of the Lowell company aroused his lieutenants and the company was hurried into line. It was the color company of the regiment, and there was also a hospital that would fall into Spanish hands if the charge was not repulsed.

The Lowell men went uphill under fire. They carried their colors and fought with the greatest cheerfulness. It was never necessary to urge them. The fight lasted for two and one-half hours, and the Spanish retired with heavy loss. Two or three members of Company M were slightly wounded, but every man was accounted for. Nobody had remained behind.

The company was complimented by General Bates and by General Wheeler. The regiment was ordered into the trenches July 3, with Lieutenant-Colonel Logan in command. Then followed days of fighting and of truce. The company learned to know the Rough Riders and their colonel. They learned to

FATHER MURPHY, Chaplain of the Ninth Massachusetts.

respect the colored troops. There were no fires because of the enemy in force in front. There was no smoking when the trenches were blazing with the rifles all day.

On the 17th of July General Toral surrendered the Spanish army. The Ninth was present at the surrender, and the Lowell company still carried the colors. Later the regiment guarded Spanish prisoners.

Then, when the excitement was all over, Company M went to pieces with sickness. The captain, suffering from the fever, was sent aboard a hospital ship, with nearly every one of his men ill in the ditches. Of the seventy-seven men who marched from Camp Dewey, only seventeen returned as a company to Lowell September 15. In groups and alone, the others were sent home from the hospitals — all but a few. The company lost by death nine men.

A STREET IN THE CAMP OF THE NINTH.

A. D. MITTEN,
Captain Company M, Ninth Regiment Infantry, Massachusetts Volunteers.

"On Fame's eternal camping ground
  Their silent tents are spread;
While Glory guards, with solemn round,
  The bivouac of the dead."

Lowell Deaths in Company M, Ninth Regiment.

CHARLES H. BRADEN, died at sea, August 29, 1898.

CHESTER F. CUMMINGS, died in New York, September 27, 1898.

JOHN E. CONNER, died at sea, August 31, 1898.

JOHN H. MARSHALL, died in Boston, September 26, 1898.

GEORGE A. PITCHER, died at sea, August 24, 1898.

WALTER SMALL, died at sea, August 27, 1898.

WALTER J. TILTON, died at sea, August 25, 1898.

RALPH B. WALKER, died in Santiago, August 1898.

JOSEPH L. WALLACE, died in Santiago, August 15, 1898.

PATRICK L. DONAHUE, Troop H, Third United States Cavalry, died in Lowell, October 10, 1898.

Deaths in the Sixth.

The following is the list of deaths in the Sixth Regiment.

LEON E. WARREN, Company H, Stoneham; died at Camp Alger.

MARTIN WELCH, Company K, Southbridge; died at Camp Alger of pneumonia.

ERNEST D. MARSHALL, Company F, Marlboro; died at Guanico of typhoid fever.

CHARLES F. PARKER, Company A, Wakefield; died in Porto Rico of typhoid fever.

WILLIS H. PAGE, Company F, Marlboro; died on the "Lampasas," on trip to Fortress Monroe, and buried at sea.

SERGEANT GEORGE C. WENDEN, Company C, Lowell; died on board hospital ship "Relief" of typhoid fever.

CHARLES E. MACGREGOR, Company K, Marlboro; died at South Framingham.

SERGEANT ASA B. TRASK, Company M, Milford; died at Adjuntas of typhoid fever.

WILLIAM A. CHUTE, Company D, Leominster; died at Ponce of typhoid fever.

A. L. WILKINSON, Company M, Milford; died at Utuado of typhoid fever.

CORPORAL HERBERT C. BELLAMY, Company C, Lowell; died at Utuado of typhoid fever.

CORPORAL RALPH P. HOSMER, Company I, Concord; died at Utuado of acute endocarditis.

CARL C. HART, Company I, Concord; died at Utuado.

JOHN E. RILEY, Company L, Boston; died at Ponce.

SERGEANT GEORGE C. WENDEN,
Company C, Sixth Regiment.

CORPORAL HERBERT C. BELLAMY,
Company C, Sixth Massachusetts.

Dirge for a Soldier.

Close his eyes; his work is done!
  What to him is friend or foeman,
Rise of moon or set of sun,
  Hand of man or kiss of woman?
    Lay him low, lay him low,
    In the clover or the snow!
    What cares he? He cannot know:
    Lay him low!

As man may, he fought his fight,
  Proved his truth by his endeavor.
Let him sleep in solemn night:
  Sleep forever and forever.
    Lay him low, lay him low,
    In the clover or the snow!
    What cares he? He cannot know:
    Lay him low!

Fold him in his country's stars,
  Roll the drum and fire the volley.
What to him are all our wars?
  What but death-bemocking folly?
    Lay him low, lay him low,
    In the clover or the snow!
    What cares he? He cannot know:
    Lay him low!

Leave him to God's watching eye,
  Trust him to the hand that made him;
Mortal love weeps idly by:
  God alone has power to aid him.
    Lay him low, lay him low,
    In the clover or the snow!
    What cares he? He cannot know:
    Lay him low!
               --George Henry Baker

Short History of the Sixth.

May 6 — Left Lowell and arrived at Framingham muster grounds, passing through Boston.
May 20 — Left Framingham for Camp Alger.
May 21 — Triumphal reception at Baltimore.
May 22 — Arrived at Camp Alger.
July 5 — Left Camp Alger.
July 7 — Arrived at Charleston, S.C.
July 8 — Sailed on the "Yale" for Santiago.
July 25 — Landed at Guanico, Porto Rico, after seventeen days aboard the "Yale," not having landed at Santiago
July 26 — Fight on the Yauco road, in which Captain Gihon was wounded. Major Darling distinguished himself for brave daring. Led by Lieutenant Butler Ames.
Aug. 1 — First companies arrived at Ponce. Colonel Henry's order for examination of efficiency of some of the Sixth's officers.
Aug. 3 — Resignation of officers.
Aug. 5 — Officers officially discharged by War Department.
Aug. 6 — Arrived at Ponce.
Aug. 8 — Colonel Edmund Rice and Lieutenant Butler Ames officially named as new officers of the regiment.
Aug. 9 — Left Ponce for Utuado. Colonel Rice in command.
Aug. 13 — Advance companies reach Utuado.
Aug. 17 — Colonel Woodward and other officers reach Boston.
Oct. 21 — Left Arecibo, Porto Rico, on the "Mississippi" for home.
Oct. 27 — Arrived in Lowell and furloughed.

LIEUTENANT-COLONEL AMES, MAJOR DARLING, and SERGEANT ANDREWS, taken on board the "Yale."

LIEUTENANT-COLONEL BUTLER AMES,
Sixth Regiment Infantry, Massachusetts Volunteers.

Garrison Duty with the Sixth in Porto Rico.

WHEN the protocol had been signed, and the three advancing columns of American troops had been brought to a sudden halt, the Sixth was high and wet at Utuado, two-thirds of the way across the Island of Porto Rico, and one short day's march from the sea at Arecibo.

Had the armistice been deferred one more day the regiment would have reached the railroad at the coast and cut off one-third of the Spanish forces on the island, preventing their retreat to San Juan. Another American column had encountered the Spanish in the western end of the island, not far from Lares, and the enemy's headlong retreat would have brought them into the town of Arecibo one day after the Sixth.

As it was, our outposts, established the night of our arrival at Utuado to prevent a possible surprise, marked the limit of the territory in "actual occupation by the American forces," and, by the terms of the armistice, marked the limit of our jurisdiction. Beyond our outposts we could not go, nor did the Spanish attempt to go beyond theirs, which were some eight miles from our own.

This left a line or belt of neutral territory, as it were, between the lines, where neither party could offer any protection to life and property.

The Spaniards, in their enforcement of military law, had disarmed the inhabitants of Spanish and Porto Rican origin, through fear of an uprising in favor of the United States by these people, who had become disgusted with misrule, and who looked forward, with ill-concealed pleasure, to the American capture and occupation of the island. But among the natives were two elements at swords' points: the so-called Spaniards, who were planters, property owners, and merchants, and the Porto Ricans, who were the working people. The latter had been the victims of the Spanish misrule, and they had been maltreated, whipped, and put in jail, and their lands swindled away to line the pockets of the "Peninsular Spanish."

So, when the Spanish arms were defeated, they felt that at last the yoke was to be taken from their necks and what was formerly their own was to come back to them; all the Spaniards must leave the island, and to that end they commenced to burn and threaten.

Plantation after plantation went up in smoke, and vengeance for generations of wrongs and injustices was wreaked by the Peons (natives) on the Spanish residents.

In the town proper we had little difficulty in keeping order. The first thing requiring attention was the sanitary condition of the streets and back yards. It was the custom to throw all kinds of refuse into the streets, and a shopkeeper felt that he was a model of neatness provided his store and sidewalk were clean.

LIEUTENANT-COLONEL BUTLER AMES.
Photograph made in Porto Rico.

An order given through the alcalde, or mayor, to the effect that this practise must stop and that the offenders would be held responsible, failed to have the desired effect, as the provost guard, being unable to talk the language, could not intelligently remonstrate. Therefore, guards were placed around the streets, and a more practical method was employed to abate the nuisance.

When any litter was found in front of a store (the store people were the chief offenders, and the nuisance was increased by the numerous small ponies that were used for travel, purchase, and delivery), a non-commissioned officer and a private or two would enter the store, call the proprietor to the door, and indicate in gestures what was desired of him.

Sometimes the wily Spaniard would feign ignorance of the object desired, until the guard, losing patience, would order the men to close the doors of the store.

Such a proceeding brought the offender around at once, and in a trice the street would be cleaned and the doors reopened.

ONE OF THE SIXTH'S WAGONS IN PORTO RICO.

Firm and insistent demands of this nature soon put the town in perfect condition and left the regiment free to do guard and drill duties. The civil authorities had a police force (called Guardia Civil) that kept the peace in the town proper, but, being closely connected with the people, could not be relied upon to stop depredations and fires in the country round about. As the Spanish residents were without arms, the native outlaws acted with impunity.

They organized into bands, of which the "Mano Negro" (black hand) became the most noted and dreaded. Owing to the absence of roads and the hilly and mountainous nature of the country, they could easily elude any pursuers, and our horses could not walk where they trotted on the small ponies of that country that had apparently developed some of the traits of a goat.

Plantation owners for miles around would come to headquarters and beg for a guard of fifteen or twenty men to repel an expected attack. This afforded the most agreeable features of

LIEUTENANT-COLONEL AMES' BODY-SERVANT, WEST.

garrison duty for the men, as the grateful planters furnished horses, food, and shelter, and opened their houses and hearts to their protectors. In no case were more than two men sent to a plantation, and then only when an attack was expected; for, while the outlaws had no fear of the Spanish owner and some ten or twenty servants, an "Americano" was looked upon as a "devil incarnate," that feared nothing, and whom nothing could hurt.

Again and again two men stood off crowds of from fifty to a hundred natives, armed with machetes and old-fashioned firearms, bent on murder, robbery, and burning.

Our men had orders to shoot to kill even people acting suspiciously, and the high-powered guns, when used on a crowd, would wound or kill as many as stood in the line of fire.

There was an element of danger and skill that strongly appealed to American men,—to be alone with a comrade eighteen or twenty miles from aid, with the outlaws' signal-fires blinking at each other across from hill to hill, with a cowering Spaniard's family and servants huddled in terror and fear, looking into the darkness, and listening for a sound or movement that showed the approach of the expected "Mano Negro," and then the crack, crack, crack of the magazine gun, a sound that is' peculiar to itself, and a stark and staring outlaw on his last rampage.

Such were the experiences that your men went through, and such were the bright spots in two months of garrison duty.

BUTLER AMES.

DRILLING RECRUITS.

CAPTAIN GREIG,
Company C, Sixth Regiment Infantry, Massachusetts Volunteers.

Data of Company C, Sixth Massachusetts Regiment.

1825. Oct. 25 — Company C, Lowell Mechanics Phalanx, organized.
1861. Civil War.
1865. Marched through Baltimore (Luther Ladd killed).
1880. Mar. 4 - Attended inauguration of President Garfield at Washington.
1896. Mar. 4 Attended inauguration of President McKinley, being the only company of the Sixth Massachusetts Regiment to attend.
1898. May 6 — Went into camp at South Framingham, Massachusetts.

May 12 — Mustered into United States Volunteer service.

May 20 — Left South Framingham for Camp Alger, Virginia.

May 22 — Marched through Baltimore.

May 23 — Arrived in Camp Alger, Virginia.

May 23 to July 6 — In camp at Camp Alger, Virginia.

July 6 — Left Camp Alger for Charleston, S. C.

July 8 Left Charleston, S. C., on board United States steamship " Yale," for Santiago, Cuba.

July 12 — Arrived off Siboney, Cuba.

July 18 — Sailed for Guantanamo Bay.

July 21 — Left Guantanamo Bay for Porto Rico.

July 25 - Arrived at Guanica, Porto Rico, and disembarked.

July 26 — Engaged in skirmish with Spaniards about four miles out of Guanica.

July 27 - In trenches at Guanica. Captain Greig given charge of the outpost, consisting of four companies.

July 27 to 29 - - Camp at Guanica.

July 29 — Marched to Yauco.

July 30 — Marched to Tallaboa.

COMPANY C, SIXTH REGIMENT INFANTRY, MASSACHUSETTS VOLUNTEERS.

July 31 — Marched to Ponce.
Aug. 1 to 9 — Camp at Ponce.
Aug. 10 — Marched to Guangnanares.
Aug. 11 — Marched to Coffee Plantation.
Aug. 12 — Marched to Adjuntas.
Aug. 14 — Marched to Utuado.
Aug. 17 — Company ordered to Lares to take same; after having marched halfway were recalled by order of General Miles.
Aug. 18 - Sergeant George C. Wenden died on board hospital ship "Relief," and was buried at sea.
Aug. 14 to 24 — Company in camp on bank of stream at Utuado, about one mile out.
Aug. 24 - Went into barracks in town of Utuado.
Aug. 24 to Sept. 16 — In barracks at Utuado.
Sept. 7 — Corporal Herbert C. Bellamy died, and was buried the same day at Utuado.
Sept. 17 — Company detached from regiment and sent to Lares to protect plantations, etc.; also to take charge of Lares, which was occupied by Spanish soldiers. Captain Greig made governor general of Lares and surrounding country.
Sept. 18 to Oct. 18 — Company in barracks at Lares. Men on outpost duty, protecting plantations.
Oct. 19 - Marched to Arecibo.
Oct. 20 — Marched to San Juan.
Oct. 21 — Left on board United States transport "Mississippi" for United States.
Oct. 28 — Arrived in Boston, Mass.
Oct. 28 — Arrived in Lowell, Mass.
Nov. 3 Furloughed by Captain Greig, Jr., until Jan. 3, 1899.
Aug. 10 — Lieutenant Costello appointed battalion adjutant.
June 23 — Corporal Pearson appointed regiment sergeant-major; afterwards made second lieutenant, Company G.
Oct. 1 — Corporal Carey appointed regiment sergeant-major.

CAPTAIN FAIRWEATHER,
Company G, Sixth Regiment Infantry, Massachusetts Volunteers.

Company G, Sixth Regiment Infantry, Massachusetts Volunteers.

ON May 6, 1898, Company G, Sixth Massachusetts Regiment, United States Volunteers, better known as "The Putnam Guards," left Lowell for the State camp ground at South Framingham, where, one week later, we were mustered into the United States service. On the 20th, in company with the regiment, we started for Camp Alger, in Virginia, taking part on the 21st in the Sixth's second march through Baltimore, and going into camp on the 22d. After six weeks of camp life, in which time we had two brigade reviews, one of them by the President in company with General Miles, and a practise march to Ball's Bluff and return, we were taken to Charleston, July 5, and sent on board the steamship "Yale" July 8, where we spent the next seventeen days. While on board the "Yale" the company was complimented by General Miles on the possession of such singers as Privates O'Brien, Iby, Halpin, and Murphy. During our stay on the "Yale" we saw the towns and historic spots of Guantanamo, Siboney, Aguadores, with its bridge, Baiquiri, and the Morro Castle of Santiago.

On the 21st of July we left the coast of Cuba behind us, and on the 25th landed at Guanica, on the south side of Porto Rico, going into camp at 6 P.M., but not for long, for at two o'clock on the 26th we were ordered out in heavy marching order, and at 6 A.M. we were ambushed by the Spaniards on the road leading to Yauco. Company G was extremely fortunate, for, although in the thickest of the fight, they brought back nothing to show for it but two bullet-pierced hats. For the remainder of the 26th and part of the 27th Company G had its share of picket duty, being stationed at a house on a hill overlooking the battle-field. Here in the building of defenses was a chance to utilize material, and Private Hunt grasped it: he and another member rolled a hollowed log of lignum-vitæ wood up on top of our earthworks, the log at a little distance resembling a field-piece of fair dimensions. On the 29th the company spent the day loading hay and grain onto the transport "Nueces," and on the 30th the regiment moved to Yauco, going to Tallaboa, in Penuelas, on the 31st, and to Ponce on the 1st day of August. After a week of resting we again moved on the 9th to Guanajarges, where the men rested their feet against their bayonets stuck in the ground, to keep themselves from sliding down hill as they slept. On the 10th we moved to Buena Vista, and on the 11th to Adjuntas, Company G on these two days acting as train guard and having the novelty of seeing ox teams and oxen attached go over the precipices, but when it came to carrying the supplies and baggage up to the road again the novelty wore off. The 13th found us on the road once more, and when we stopped this time it was in Utuado, a town that was our existing place for nine long weeks, and one that will be remembered by the men for some time.

Here, also, we left one of our townsmen, although not a member of our company, — Corporal Bellamy, of Company C. On the 8th of September a letter from General Garrettson, brigade commander, was received and read to the company. In it he complimented the regiment very highly for its efficiency and good behavior. On the 13th of October we moved from Utuado, and after the longest and one of the roughest marches of the campaign arrived in Arecibo, only to be ordered to Bayamon on the following day. Utilizing the railroad that runs along the coast here, it took but three hours to cover a two days' march, and at 7 P.M., on the 14th, we were the farthest east of any company of the Sixth, and on the 15th, when the stars and stripes were raised, the company had the distinction of taking possession of the town nearest the capital, Bayamon being only five miles from San Juan. On the 19th we left Bayamon, and on the 21st the steamship "Mississippi" carried us out of San Juan harbor, past El Morro, where the red and yellow no longer floats, and towards those shores which we all were longing to reach. The 27th, at 9 A.M., brought Boston to our sight, and it was but a few hours later when we were once more among our friends and relatives, very well able to appreciate the old song, "Home Again."

COMPANY G, SIXTH REGIMENT INFANTRY, MASSACHUSETTS VOLUNTEERS.

COLONEL ROOSEVELT.

Roosevelt.

YOUR impression of Theodore Roosevelt is correct. Everybody's is. There is no inside view of him. The public man is the private man, and his friends have no advantage in acquaintance with him over strangers. On the contrary, most people who have never met him call him "Teddy." His friends never do that, not even behind his back, neither among themselves nor in their hearts when alone. They are intimate with him; strangers only are familiar.

The Rough Riders called him by his nickname at Tampa, but at Montauk he was always "The Colonel." It is said the change occurred about the time of that charge up San Juan Hill. He went wet and cold and hot and hungry with them after that, so they all must have got nearer together and much better acquainted. Yet they became respectful as their affection grew.

It is all a mere matter of realization, however. His troopers did not bring back any new conception of him. He is brave, strong, fair, and happy—and they knew that when they joined the regiment. But when they saw what it meant to be so, when they watched with the eye what they had seen long before with the mind, they knew better what they knew. That was all, and it had happened just so before.

His is a peculiarly American personality—as picturesque and national as Lincoln's or Grant's, though he, unlike them, was born in the "upper" classes. His very pedigree is distinctly American, for it is almost equally made up of Dutch, French, Scotch, and Irish elements. He is one of the cloud of witnesses to the productivity of Harvard. It was there that he combated the ill health of his early boyhood and made himself a champion at boxing and a polo captain. He then went to Europe and earned a membership in the Alpine Club by climbing the Matterhorn and the Jungfrau.

At twenty-five he was in the West hunting big game and participating in one of the last great buffalo hunts. Returning to New York, he joined the Eighth Regiment of the New York National Guard, and at thirty was captain. Meanwhile, he was up to his eyes in politics, fighting the boss of his district and getting himself sent to the Assembly at the age of twenty-four. There, too, he was a reformer, none the less practical for his enthusiasm. He was the Republican candidate for mayor of New York city at the age of twenty-eight, and, though he was beaten, he polled a larger vote in proportion to the total than any Republican had ever received. He was made a member of the Civil Service Commission by President Harrison, and retained by President Cleveland, resigning to become the president of the Police Board of New York under Mayor Strong's reform administration. His absolute conscientiousness and his characteristic pugnacity gave that administration a national interest. Next he appeared as the Assistant Secretary of the Navy, and threw extraordinary energy into the preparation for war with Spain, leaving the desk for the field at the beginning of hostilities. The magic of his name as second in command brought ten thousand candidates for the one regiment of Rough Riders that was known as Roosevelt's, though he refused to accept the colonelcy of it till he won it by a superb display of courage under fire.

All this while Colonel Roosevelt has mingled scholarship and letters with his activities, writing frequent magazine articles and numerous books, not only volumes on big game hunting for the sportsman, but famous works on the making of the West for the student of our institutions, a standard naval history, and two ideal biographies. In everything he has evinced that sturdy democracy, that unimpeached honor, that irrepressible zest for life and activity that should characterize the man of letters most of all, though it seems usually to mark him least; and, all in all, the Spanish war has brought to no personality so much prestige as it has bestowed on Colonel Theodore Roosevelt.

The Song of the Camp.

"Give us a song!" the soldiers cried,
  The outer trenches guarding,
When the heated guns of the camps allied
  Grew weary of bombarding.

The dark Redan, in silent scoff,
  Lay, grim and threatening, under;
And the tawny mound of the Malakoff
  No longer belched its thunder.

There was a pause. A guardsman said:
  "We storm the forts tomorrow;
Sing while we may, another day
  Will bring enough of sorrow."

They lay along the battery's side,
  Below the smoking cannon;
Brave hearts from Severn and from Clyde,
  And from the banks of Shannon.

They sang of love and not of fame;
  Forgot was Britain's glory.
Each heart recalled a different name,
  But all sang "Annie Laurie."

Voice after voice caught up the song,
  Until its tender passion
Rose like an anthem rich and strong—
  Their battle-eve confession.

Dear girl, her name he dared not speak,
  But, as the song grew louder,
Something upon the soldier's cheek
  Washed off the stains of powder.

Beyond the darkening ocean burned
  The bloody sunset's embers,
While the Crimean valleys learned
  How English love remembers.

And once again a fire of hell
  Rained on the Russian quarters
With scream of shot, and burst of shell,
  And bellowing of the mortars.

And Irish Nora's eyes are dim
  For a singer, dumb and gory,
And English Mary mourns for him
  Who sang of "Annie Laurie."

Sleep, soldiers! still in honored rest
  Your truth and valor wearing;
The bravest are the tenderest,
  The loving are the daring. — *Bayard Taylor.*

Hon. CHARLES H. ALLEN,
Assistant Secretary of the Navy.

NAVY DEPARTMENT.

WASHINGTON, Nov. 25, 1898.

My Dear Mr. Mayor:

I wish I could personally join with you in the welcome the citizens of Lowell are to extend to the soldiers and sailors of this war; but that is not permitted me.

The experience these men have gained during the past six months will always be a pride and satisfaction to them, and their eagerness to serve upon the first intimation of need reflects credit upon them and upon our city, where, we are glad always to remember, rest the remains of those who first laid down their lives in the War of the Rebellion.

You ask me to say something about the Navy. The truth is, at the Department we devote our attention to the daily duties and allow the Navy to speak for itself. That it has done so most emphatically none will deny.

Sometimes people, without thinking, have spoken of the "luck" of the Navy. I can truthfully say there has been mighty little "luck" in the matter, unless it be that "luck" which is apt to attend an enterprise which is always and continuously looked after so carefully that the smallest detail is not omitted.

The fact is that from the time the good sense of Congress asserted itself in a determination to build up a new navy there has not been a day upon any United States ship in commission which has not been devoted to preparation for just such an exigency as presented itself at the beginning of this war. Contrary to a somewhat general impression, the daily routine on board ship in time of peace is an interminable hourly drill, all in line of what would actually happen in case of war. So, when the order came to Admiral Dewey at Hong Kong on the 24th of April to "Proceed at once, capture Spanish vessels, or destroy," there was not an instant's delay in execution.

And in the exciting events which followed in quick succession the strength and quality of the system of preparation were amply demonstrated.

History will show how well the work of the Department was carried on. From the proclamation of war to the signing of the protocol no time was lost in parades or useless red tape. Ordnance, equipment, engineering, construction, navigation,—all the great bureaus worked in complete harmony, and from the head of the department throughout the entire personnel the only rivalry was as to who could best serve.

The Department was never closed during the war—night or day, Sundays or holidays.

But I cannot speak of the Navy without being irresistibly drawn to speak of its commander-in-chief, President McKinley. I have been near him during almost the entire period of the war, and from that personal experience I speak from conviction when I say I am sure no President of this country ever gave more self-sacrificing, devoted service to the people than he. His work has been continuous, absolutely without rest or recreation of any sort. From early morning until far into the night the hours have been filled with earnest effort to accomplish whatever led to honor and progress for his country. His ideals have been high; his actions and his speeches upon the loftiest plane, and his sympathetic tenderness to all suffering has never been wanting when appealed to. He intuitively sees the large meaning of things, and bends details to their accomplishment. How in the world the man has stood up under it all I cannot say, though I believe through it all he has been sustained by a higher power, which has given him wisdom and strength and firmness.

All this is known, of course; but no one who has been intimately connected with affairs in Washington during the interesting period of the Spanish War can help saying these things of the President, because he knows the self-sacrificing devotion of this officer, who has endeared himself to the hearts of his countrymen.

The immediate direction of the Navy centered, of course, in the head of the Department, where our friend and neighbor, Governor Long, whom everybody in Massachusetts loves and honors, was in control. Governor Long brought to the Department great executive ability, capacity for work, honesty, and those qualities which always command confidence and admiration.

Modest man as he is, his report will be sure to give praise and honor to others; but he deserves it for himself. He has been, in fact as in name, the head of the Department, and whatever credit attaches to it will always be associated, so far as this war is concerned, with his administration. Massachusetts may well be proud of her contribution to the head of that Department during the war.

And I might go on, for in an experience covering quite a

ADMIRAL GEORGE DEWEY.

period in public life and in business experience I have never seen greater devotion to duty than has animated the entire personnel of the Navy.

Their work was well done, and the victories of Manila Bay and Santiago will go down to history as among the most marvelous of naval engagements; and so long as the names of Dewey and Sampson and Schley and Hobson (and our own townsman, Charette) are remembered, so long will our people turn with generous pride to the story and the deeds of the American Navy.

Very truly yours,

(Signed) CHAS. H. ALLEN.

HON. JAS. W. BENNETT, Mayor,
    City Hall, Lowell, Mass.

THE SUNKEN "MERRIMACK."

GEORGE CHARETTE,
of Lowell, who went with Hobson on the "Merrimack."

Hon. JAS. W. BENNETT,
Mayor of Lowell.

The Personal Efforts of Lowell's Mayor and His Assistants for the Comfort and Care of Lowell's Soldiers.

*I*N the month of June the State of Massachusetts voted to pay State aid to those entirely dependent upon the soldier, sailor, or marine who enlisted in the service of the United States to the credit of the Commonwealth of Massachusetts in the war with Spain.

Lowell furnished Companies C and G of the Sixth and Company M of the Ninth Regiments, which reported at Camp Dewey, South Framingham, Mass. The State Aid Law coming under the State Aid Department, Mr. H. M. Potter, the head of the department, having all his office could do at the time, asked me to assist him in getting records of the men before they left, that it might save the city a great deal of time and money in looking up applications later. I visited the camp and procured a complete record. We also kept in touch with the recruiting offices in Boston and Lowell; and for these reasons we believe the State Aid Department has a fairly accurate list of enlistment of Lowell men.

On August 20 the mayor called me into his office and asked me if I would be his representative on receiving returning soldiers. After consulting General Dimon it was decided to have me take hold. I immediately had Mayor Bennett give me a pretty broad "To whom it may concern" that I represented the city of Lowell. I immediately went to Boston and had an interview with Governor Wolcott; got an endorsement from him, also one from Adjutant-General Dalton. I then went to the Massachusetts Volunteer Aid Association and got letters which gave me free use of everything of theirs anywhere in the country and letters of introduction to their representatives at all points. Armed with such credentials, my way has been easy and pleasant.

The first duty I had was in caring for the six sick ones of the Ninth Regiment that arrived on the Massachusetts hospital boat "Bay State" on the thirtieth of August from Santiago. I was at the boat, spoke with the soldiers as they came off, went to the hospital, and saw the men comfortable. Then I came to Lowell at night, took a carriage, and visited all their families and told them the exact condition of their sons or husbands. I revisited the hospitals, and then went to Montauk Point via Massachusetts Volunteer boat from New London. I found there that the Ninth was in Detention Camp, and strongly guarded. I presented myself to General Wheeler, in command, showed him my credentials, and received from him a pass to go everywhere on the grounds; but his advice was not to enter the Detention Hospital.

I first visited Detention Camp, and the boys were very glad to see me. After a consultation with Major Donovan and Lieutenant McNulty I made a tour of the General Hospital, and looked up the Lowell boys. I then went to the Detention Hospital, and found but two Lowell boys, although, in company with Dr. Hughes, I visited every cot in the hospital. I then returned to camp and told the boys where their associates were, having found in the General Hospital where the balance were, — in New York and Brooklyn hospitals.

I then came back to Lowell, and met the relatives of the soldiers at City Hall, and told them the condition of the soldiers. I immediately left again for Montauk and the New York and Brooklyn hospitals, which I visited. I saw every Lowell boy on this trip, and carried letters from relatives to a number of them. I also assorted the mail at Montauk, and carried the letters that had accumulated to the boys in the hospitals. In all the hospitals I left orders to have everything done for the Lowell boys and to have bills for expense incurred sent to me. I then returned to Lowell and reported the condition of everybody. I immediately went to Boston, and found Black, Early, and Laing in condition to come home. I had a carriage, took them to Quartermaster Hyde, and had them fitted out with clothing; brought them to Lowell, and left them at their homes. The members of the Ninth that were able then returned from Montauk and gave us a great deal to do here, as a great many of them became sick at once on arrival home. I was going to Boston and New York hospitals all the time I had to spare.

I found that a number of the members of the Ninth Regiment had allotted their State pay of seven dollars per month to themselves, but were unable to go to Boston to get it. I made arrangements with State Treasurer Shaw to allow the Traders National Bank, which kindly volunteered, to make collections free and to do collecting for them; and it has been a great benefit to a lot of them who needed it.

We next find the hospital ship "Bay State" coming from Porto Rico with the sick of the Sixth Regiment; there being such an anxious feeling on the part of the folks at home to have their

boys brought directly to Lowell, I had arranged before the arrival
of the boat with Dr. Bradford, who had absolute control, to have
all Lowell men possible sent home. He agreed, if I could arrange
furloughs and easy transportation. I arranged with Lieutenant
Ashbourne, furloughing officer at Boston, so that when the

OFFICERS COMMISSIONED BY GOVERNOR WOLCOTT.

"Bay State" arrived Dr. Bradford, who had gone to quarantine
to meet it, sent me the Lowell men with a card with an "L"
on. I had three carriages, with an ambulance man detailed to
each, waiting at the wharf. I took Lieutenant Ashbourne in a

carriage, and we went to Boston City Hospital. Our three carriages followed. He gave us the preference. As soon as all were furloughed we came to the depot, where a special car was in waiting. At Lowell we were met by his honor at the Merrimack Street Station, where carriages and ambulance were in waiting. We brought sixteen on this trip, leaving Private Trembly, of Company C, at the Massachusetts General Hospital, the doctor not thinking him able to travel that night. I immediately left that night for New York, to bring back the body of Chester F. Cummings, of Company M, who had died that day at St. Francis Xavier Hospital. I returned with the body on the three o'clock train that afternoon.

On September 29 we had the funeral of John H. Marshall, of Company M, from St. Peter's Church; on the 30th we had the funeral of Chester F. Cummings, of Company M, from the Central Methodist-Episcopal Church. They took a great deal of time, as the city was represented, and bore most of the arrangements.

Lieutenants Gillow and McNulty, of Company M, having been left at Montauk Point, the natural anxiety of many friends caused me to make numerous trips to New London with the Massachusetts Volunteer Aid Association, to keep in touch with them in case they came home.

Patrick E. Donahoe, of Troop H, Third United States Cavalry, a Lowell boy, died at St. John's Hospital October 10. He was buried from the Immaculate Conception Church October 12, the city government attending.

We next have the Sixth Regiment "home-coming" from Porto Rico. I was detailed to watch the Boston end and to keep Lowell posted. As a result of combined efforts, I think the reception will go down in history as the greatest success Lowell ever had in that line.

The next day the hospital boat "Bay State" arrived again with twenty-eight Lowell boys of companies C and G. As the Boston hospitals were pretty full, I had arranged with our hospitals to take forty-five of the one hundred and thirteen that came, if necessary, but, after consultation with Dr. Bradford, it was found unnecessary. We brought twenty-three of the twenty-eight Lowell boys to Lowell, the other five being too weak to move the extra distance. We had a special car, equipped with nurses, bouillon, coffee, and light refreshments. We were met at the Merrimac Street Station by his honor, with carriages, as before.

All the spare time I have had in Lowell I have visited the sick from day to day, to see that they wanted for nothing. We now have all members of Companies C, G, and M returned to Lowell, except Sylvester L. Lane, of Company M, Ninth, who is in Carney Hospital, Boston; Francis W. McGlynn, Joseph Delorme, of Company C, and John S. Brophy, of Company G, who were left at Porto Rico.

I think this gives a brief account of what I have done. It has meant a great deal of hard work for me, night and day, for ten weeks. I have been greatly assisted by the Ladies' Auxiliary Aid Association, Dr. T. F. Harrington, who has accompanied me on all trips to Boston to meet the "Bay State," and Frank W. Hall, the mayor's private secretary. Words can never express what I know His Honor J. W. Bennett, mayor, has done during all this work.

ARTHUR F. SALMON.

In this connection the following copies of correspondence will be found interesting :

LOWELL, MASS., Aug. 22, 1898.

CAPTAIN A. D. MITTEN,

    Company M, Ninth Massachusetts Volunteers,

        Camp Wikoff, Montauk Point, L. I.

MY DEAR CAPTAIN :

As I learn from the papers that your company will soon be on home soil, I would like to be prepared to see them taken care of and that they may want for nothing that can make them comfortable. I thought you might be able to let me know what some of their wants will be in advance, and would be very glad to receive suggestions from you.

Please let me know at your earliest convenience what disposition is to be made of your company.

Very respectfully,

J. W. BENNETT, Mayor.

His Excellency ROGER WOLCOTT,
State House, Boston, Mass.

My Dear Sir:

Now that the Second and the Ninth Regiments have returned, we are anxious about our two companies, C and G, in the Sixth Regiment. There are a great many married men in these two companies, and their families are making daily inquiries as to when they will return. It is the earnest wish of the Lowell people that the Sixth may be home again soon, and I would be greatly pleased if you could obtain for me any information in relation to their home-coming.

Very respectfully yours,
J. W. BENNETT, Mayor.

COMMONWEALTH OF MASSACHUSETTS.
Executive Department.

Boston, Aug. 30, 1898.

Hon. J. W. BENNETT, Mayor.
Lowell, Mass.

My Dear Sir:

In reply to your letter of August 29 regarding the return of the Sixth Massachusetts Infantry, United States Volunteers, I have the honor to say that I am informed by the Secretary of War that the United States will retain in its service for the present a certain number of the Massachusetts Volunteer Regiments. The Second and Ninth, having suffered so severely through battle and disease, will be mustered out at an early day, and the ultimate selection of the regiments that shall remain in the service rests with the War Department. As to the length of additional service which will be asked of these latter regiments I have no certain information, although the indications would seem to point to a somewhat early discharge.

Very truly yours,
ROGER WOLCOTT.

Dr. G. H. M. ROWE,
  Superintendent City Hospital,
    Boston, Mass.
My Dear Sir:

Whenever any Lowell men in your hospital are to be transferred to some other hospital, we would like to arrange with you to have them sent to Lowell hospitals, where there are now upwards of twenty beds at their disposal. We think up here that it would be a good deal better to move these men to Lowell than it would be to send them off to some other place.

If this proposition meets your approval, will you please notify me a sufficient time in advance when you contemplate moving any Lowell men, and I will send my representative down to escort them to Lowell?

  Very respectfully yours,
    J. W. BENNETT, Mayor.

  Lowell, Mass., Oct. 3, 1898.
Gen. C. A. R. DIMON,
  Chairman Board of Aldermen,
    Lowell, Mass.
My Dear Sir:

You, as Chairman of the Board of Aldermen of the city of Lowell, are hereby authorized and directed to go immediately to Porto Rico, W. I., and make careful investigation into the condition and needs of the soldiers belonging to the city of Lowell, in Companies C and G, of the Sixth Massachusetts Volunteers. Please report to me at the earliest possible moment after your arrival at Porto Rico upon what you may find, and suggest what in your judgment should be done in regard to the better care of the sick and wounded, the sending home of those who are incapacitated and can be moved, and also in regard to the general welfare of all the Lowell men in the field.

  Very respectfully yours,
    J. W. BENNETT, Mayor.

Executive Committee on Banquet.

ALFRED E. ROSE, Chairman.
HON. J. W. BENNETT.
J. L. CHALIFOUX.
REV. GEO. F. KENNGOTT.
ASA C. RUSSELL.
COLONEL A. M. CHADWICK, Chairman Reception Committee.
C. I. HOOD, Chairman Entertainment Committee.
JAMES S. HASTINGS, Chairman Decoration Committee.
C. L. McCLEERY, Chairman Advertising Committee.
CAPTAIN CHARLES H. KIMBALL, Chief Marshal.
FRANK W. HALL, Secretary.

"I have but one sentiment for soldiers living or dead: cheers for the living, tears for the dead."

The editor of this souvenir acknowledges with warmest thanks his indebtedness to the "Boston Journal," "Ainslee's Magazine," the "Review of Reviews," for the use of matter and illustrations; W. J. Freeman and F. H. Pearson for the loan of photographs; and G. R. Halm, the artist, for original drawings.

www.ingramcontent.com/pod-product-compliance
Lightning Source LLC
Chambersburg PA
CBHW020325090426
42735CB00009B/1409